Word Warriors

Write like an Author – Course Book Three

Brian Falkner

Falkner Books
2016

This edition published in 2016 by

Falkner Books

Copyright © 2016 by Brian Falkner

Illustrations by Ron Leishman
Some images in this publication used under 'Fair Use' for educational purposes

On the web at:
brianfalkner.com
writelikeanauthor.com

All rights reserved. This book or any portion thereof may not be reproduced or used in any manner whatsoever without the express written permission of the publisher except for the use of brief quotations in a book review or scholarly journal.

First Printing: 2016

ISBN 978-0-9944567-2-4

Are you ready to rumble?

It's game day!

Now is the time to start the actual writing.

A lot of people seem to think that writing is hard. Here's what I think:

I think most people who want to write stories just sit down at their computer and start writing.

Can you imagine if you tried to play chess that way? If you just sat down at a chess-board and started moving pieces around without first learning the rules of the game. Or if you tried to play football or basketball by running out onto a field or a court without practising the moves and learning the plays.

Of course it would be hard. Anything would be hard if you tried to do it that way.

So in this book I am going to teach you how to play the game of 'writing'. I am going to show you the moves, teach you the rules, and coach you through the plays.

You want to write like a pro? Write like an author? Here is where I show you how.

Happy writing!

Brian

MY FAVOURITE BOOKS

A lot of people ask me what my favourite books are. Well here are a few:

Dune
*by Frank Herbert
IMHO the best science fiction novel ever written.*

Matilda
*by Roald Dahl
I love Roald Dahl books and this is my favourite.*

Five On A Treasure Island
*by Enid Blyton
When I was young, nothing beat the excitement of a new Famous Five book to read. This was the first, and one of the best.*

Where Eagles Dare
*by Alistair Maclean
It's hard for me to pick any one of Maclean's books, but this is definitely a favourite. Suspense, treachery, plot twists and great action.*

Battlesaurus: Rampage at Waterloo
*by Me
Sorry for including one of my own novels. but if I hadn't written this book, it would still be one of my favourites.*

The Framework

Let's start by breaking down writing into its component parts: the *Framework* of Writing.

There are four parts to the Framework:
1. Narration
2. Description
3. Dialogue & Action
4. Inner thoughts

Each has its own, very important part to play in good creative writing, yet often I read stories which are almost all narration, or all dialogue. A good story should contain a mix of all four parts.

There are of course exceptions. You may well have read stories which were entirely made up of dialogue, or email messages, or all narration.

When you are a famous author you can break any rules you like. But for now it is important to learn the rules.

> Learn the rules like a pro, so you can break them like an artist.
> – Pablo Picasso

BRIAN SAYS

I first learned about the framework of writing from the famous horror author Stephen King.

It was the first time I had seen something so simple that explained what creative writing was all about.

It opened my eyes and I hope it will open your eyes too.

The Framework

Narration
This moves the story from A to B. This is you, the author, telling the reader stuff they need to know. It's the bare bones of the story without any of the embellishments that make up good creative writing.

Description
Good description puts the reader into the story. It makes them feel they are really there by creating a 'sensory reality'. You describe the scene using a number of senses, to make it real for the reader.

Dialogue & Action
You use dialogue and action to make your characters come to life, saying and doing stuff. It also brings the story to life because things are happening.

Inner Thoughts
For the reader to really empathise with the character, they need to know what is going in inside their head, and inside their heart.

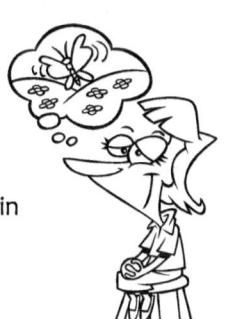

On the next page there is a short excerpt of a story, broken down into its component parts, to help clarify the framework.

THE RULE OF THREE

Occasionally I will talk about the rule of three. This is a good principle to follow in writing.

Doing things in threes can be more effective and more satisfying than just one, or two.

That's why so many jokes use the rule of three. (An Englishman, an American and an Australian walk into a bar... etc)

It's also why there are three little pigs, three bears in Goldilocks, three Billy Goats Gruff and so on and so on.

Kornfeld Story (Narration Only)

> I was sitting alone in the old hall when Kornfeld walked in, saw me and demanded that I give him my lunch.

That's it. Not much to it is there? Still we can learn quite a lot from this short excerpt. One of the characters is clearly a loner. He is sitting alone at lunchtime, in a deserted old school hall. The other character seems like a bully.

That's about it. But watch what happens when we add **description** to the **narration.**

Kornfeld (+ Description)

> I sat on the edge of the stage in the hall. Not the shiny, glass-walled new hall over by the communications building, but the original wooden hall, that now doubled as a gym, built when the school was built.
>
> It was filled with long hard seats, polished wood on metal frames, but old, and cracked on the edges, to drive small splinters into the legs of small boys.
>
> Light came from high, slatted windows, one of which was cracked and the wind outside made a frightened squeal through it.
>
> The place smelled of sweat, and the wet socks of hundreds of kids. That smelly socky gymmy smell that gets in your nostrils and sets up camp.
>
> Kornfeld entered. His shirt was torn across the shoulders and his trousers were too short.
>
> Half way down the aisle he demanded that I give him my lunch.

That really changes things, doesn't it? It puts you, the reader, into the scene, so you know what it is like to be there. We also learn more about the characters: Kornfeld's shirt is torn and he has outgrown his trousers. That gives us some clues to who he really is.

BRIAN SAYS

Look at the senses I used. I followed the **Rule of Three** with:

- Sight
- Sound
- Hearing

Look also at the kinds of descriptions I created with those senses.

The *cracked windows*.

The *frightened squeal* of the wind.

The *smelly socky gymmy smell*.

You need to match the kind of description to the mood of the story.

More about that later.

Kornfeld (+ Dialog & Action)

I sat on the edge of the stage in the hall. Not the shiny, glass-walled new hall over by the communications building, but the original wooden hall, that now doubled as a gym, built when the school was built.

It was filled with long hard seats, polished wood on metal frames, but old, and cracked on the edges, to drive small splinters into the legs of small boys.

Light came from high, slatted windows, one of which was cracked and the wind outside made a frightened squeal through it.

The place smelled of sweat, and the wet socks of hundreds of kids. That smelly socky gymmy smell that gets in your nostrils and sets up camp.

Kornfeld entered with a thud as the door slammed back against the frame. His shirt was torn across the shoulders and his trousers were too short.

I tried to shrink into the gloom on the stage.

"Hey, it's the professor," his eyes lit up. He advanced down the aisle like a rumbling earthquake, pushing aside seats that he felt were in his way or just annoyed him for some reason.

"Giz your lunch, four-eyes, or I'll smash ya."

I waited until he was right in front of me, taller than me even though I was sitting up on the stage.

"Your ma forgot yours again, huh?"

"You don't talk about my mum," he seemed to grow bigger as he spoke. "You…"

I cut him off. "I got an egg-salad sammy that I don't like. You can have that. And me apple. But you gots to say please."

Do you see how the characters come to life when you give them a voice, and something to do? We learn much more about them.

Kornfeld is clearly very sensitive about his family situation. Why might that be?

The narrator, although afraid of Kornfeld, refuses to allow himself to be intimidated. He stands up to the bully.

BRIAN SAYS

Look at the speech patterns in this story.

The way the characters talk and the kind of words they use.

This is what we call the character's *voice*.

What can you deduce about each character from their *voice*?

Why does Kornfeld say things like "giz your lunch"?

Why does he call the professor "four-eyes" and "the professor".

Why does the narrator use the word "ma" instead of mum or mom?

Why does he say "gots" instead of "got" or "gotta"?

What about "Me apple" instead of "My apple"?

Kornfeld (+ Inner Thoughts)

I sat on the edge of the stage in the hall. Not the shiny, glass-walled new hall over by the communications building, but the original wooden hall, that now doubled as a gym, built when the school was built.

It was filled with long hard seats, polished wood on metal frames, but old, and cracked on the edges, to drive small splinters into the legs of small boys. Light came from high, slatted windows, one of which was cracked and the wind outside made a frightened squeal through it. The place smelled of sweat, and the wet socks of hundreds of kids. That smelly socky gymmy smell that gets in your nostrils and sets up camp.

It was a perfect place to get away from the aliens that inhabited this school. Except I knew that was wrong. They weren't the aliens. I was. Whatever reasons my olds had for coming to this country, they weren't good enough. These kids and I had nothing in common.

Kornfeld entered with a thud as the door slammed back against the frame. His shirt was torn across the shoulders and his trousers were too short. He had outgrown them again last summer I guess. I tried to shrink into the gloom on the stage, but I knew that was never going to work.

"Hey, it's the professor," his eyes lit up, but it wasn't happiness to see me, I was sure of that. He advanced down the aisle like a rumbling earthquake, pushing aside seats that he felt were in his way or just annoyed him for some reason.

"Giz your lunch, four-eyes, or I'll smash ya."

Not this time, I thought. Not this time. If I let this monster push me around again, that would set the tone of the rest of my life. At least at this school. I waited until he was right in front of me, taller than me even though I was sitting up on the stage.

"Your ma forgot yours again, huh?"

His mother didn't forget his lunch. His mother couldn't be bothered. Everybody knew that. In a way I felt sorry for him.

"You don't talk about my mum," he seemed to grow bigger as he spoke. "You…"

This was the moment. My one chance to be me, or I'd be running and hiding forever.

I cut him off. "I got an egg-salad sammy that I don't like. You can have that. And me apple. But you gots to say please."

BRIAN SAYS

Let's compare this with our original 'narration only' version of the story. Here it is:

I was sitting alone in the old hall when Kornfeld walked in, saw me and demanded that I give him my lunch.

Quite an amazing difference, I am sure you will agree. And that's really all there is to it. You combine the four parts of the framework, and suddenly a story starts to shine out of your words.

By the way, I stole the name 'Kornfeld' for this story from a writer friend of mine in New Zealand, Stina Kornfeld. She's lovely and certainly not a bully at all!

The Framework - Exercise

Here's an excerpt from *The Super Freak*.
Find four different coloured highlighter pens.
Highlight the NARRATION in one colour and the DESCRIPTION a different colour.
DIALOGUE and ACTION a third colour. INNER THOUGHTS in another colour.
Notice the pattern that it makes. It is a mixture of colours, not big long sections of a single colour. That's what your story should look like when it is finished.

I have completed this exercise, you can find it at: **http://bit.ly/SuperFreakExc**
but please do the exercise yourself before finding my version.

Gumbo ran, and I ran, and Ben ran with me, and somewhere in front of us all was Blocker.

Rain pelted us, and lightning lit the rapidly approaching night. Without raincoats we were soaked in seconds. It was freezing and miserable. Rain ran down the back of our necks and lashed at our eyes.

Objects took on strange shapes through wet, squinty eyes, trees became monsters and the wind turned branches into grasping, desperate arms. Even the hill fought us, rising up in steep little jabs, slippery with the rain.

Gumbo was surprisingly quick for an old dog, but his legs could not hold out and eventually he just stopped and looked back waiting for us to catch him up.

"Where's Blocker going?" I shouted, holding on to Gumbo's collar, but I think I already knew.

"The pylon!" Ben confirmed my thoughts, and just then lightning cracked its way across the sky nearby, follow soon after by rolling thunder.

"Get after him," Erica yelled, her hair in her eyes.

I hesitated.

"Get after him," she repeated. "You can't just leave him!"

She grabbed Gumbo's collar out of my hand, and said "I'll bring your dog."

We ran. Wind burned cold daggers into my legs and my lungs were beginning to gasp for air. Beside me, Ben ran effortlessly, mechanically, tirelessly, robotically.

By the time we had got to the top of Manuka Ridge my chest was burning and my guts were retching, Blocker had indeed turned into Ridge Road, towards the pylon.

Something about that scared me in a way I hadn't been scared before and my legs found new strength.

Lightning cracked again, and thunder drummed all around us a few seconds later. It was close.

"Three seconds!" Ben shouted into my ear. "Just three kilometers away!"

The pylon stood, sentry like, in its empty grassy field. Up this close I could see that its mighty legs were set into huge concrete blocks. It soared into the sky above us, impossibly tall when viewed from its base.

About six metres up the pylon, completely encircling it, was a horizontal fence of barbed wire, jutting sideways out from the structure to prevent anyone from climbing it.

Blocker was clinging to the tower, a dark figure, just below the barbs of the barrier.

Lighting flared again. "Two seconds!" Ben shouted.

Narration

Now we'll go into a bit more detail about the various parts of the framework. The first thing to know about **narration** is to avoid having too much of it.

We talked about **'Show, don't tell'** briefly in the *Heroes and Villains* workbook. Here it is in a nutshell:

Narration = Telling

Dialogue/Action & Description = Showing

Showing is almost always better than **telling**.

Look at this example from Kornfeld.
I could simply **tell** you something.

> Kornfeld was a bully who often stole my lunch.

But it is better when I **show** you.

> Kornfeld entered with a thud as the door slammed back against the frame. His shirt was torn across the shoulders and his trousers were too short.
> I tried to shrink into the gloom on the stage.
> "Hey, it's the professor," his eyes lit up. He advanced down the aisle like a rumbling earthquake, pushing aside seats that he felt were in his way or just annoyed him for some reason.
> "Giz your lunch, four-eyes, or I'll smash ya."

Have a look back at your Character / Trait / Action chart from the previous workbook. Make sure you show the reader who your character is, don't tell them.

*Don't tell me the moon is shining.
Show me the glint of light on broken glass.*
- Anton Chekhov

TELL, DON'T SHOW

Although it is better to **show** than to **tell**, there are times when it is the opposite. To keep your story moving, sometimes you want a bit of narration to just tell the reader what happened.

if Eric and Julia drove to the beach, but nothing of any importance happened on the way, just tell the reader this.

Eric and Julia drove to the beach.

Once they get there you can show what they **did**, what they **said**, you can **describe** the warmth of sun, the cool of the sea and the softness of the sand under their toes.

But don't **show** the reader every little unimportant event or detail or you will drive them nuts and the story will be far too long!

Use narration when you need to keep your story moving.

Show, Don't Tell *Exercise*

Take one of these three character descriptions.

1. **Honest John was the least honest person in the world.**

2. **Karinne was everybody's best friend. But not mine.**

3. **My dog ain't too smart.**

Use action, dialogue and a little description to reveal the nature of the person (or dog) instead of telling the reader about them. Think of something they could do that would show their character. Something they could say. Something about the way they look.

Use the **rule of three**. It could be two actions, one piece of dialogue, or one description, one action, one dialogue.

....
....
....
....
....
....
....
....
....
....

Now share it with your writing buddy. Do they get the sense of what you are trying to say about the character?

BRIAN SAYS

Look at this example from my book *The Flea Thing*. The main character, Daniel, has been invited to a try-out for the Warriors rugby-league team. What does it tell you about Daniel's friend Jason?

———

I had been up since six, too excited to sleep. Then, when we were getting ready to go, I couldn't find my rugby boots. I had started to panic for a moment, but just then there was a knock on the front door and Jason had shown up with them.

He had taken them the previous day without telling me and cleaned them carefully, every inch, with a toothbrush.

Then he had polished them blacker than black. When I put them on at the Warriors' training ground they had shone like a pair of brand new boots.

I said thanks to Jason, but that didn't seem like a big enough word somehow.

Description

Of all the different parts of the framework, description is perhaps the most difficult. Too little and the reader does not get immersed in the story. Too simple and the story lacks colour and life. Too flowery and you will get accused of writing 'purple prose.'

FIVE SENSES
- Sight
- Hearing
- Smell
- Taste
- Touch (or feeling)

Good description should make the reader feel like they are really there, without drawing attention to itself. If the reader starts noticing how clever your descriptive passages are, then you have pushed them away from the actual story.

Description is all about creating a "Sensory Reality" for the reader. That means making the scene seem real, using the senses. Apply the *rule of three*. **Use three senses to describe a scene.**

Think about where you are right now.

What can you see? Is it bright or dark where you are? Where is the light coming from?
What can you hear? Listen carefully to every little sound, whether inside the room where you are, or outside the window or door.
What can you feel? Is it warm, is it cold. Can you feel a breeze? Are there any other physical sensations on your skin?
What can you smell? Are there any distinct odours? Does your room smell dry, or musty?
What can you taste? That might depend on where you are and what you last ate. But if you were at the beach, for example, you might be able to taste the salt of the ocean. If you were in a fight, you might be able to taste blood on your tongue.

> *Description begins in the writer's imagination, but should finish in the reader's.*
> *– Stephen King*

Feeling it!

Now we need to take your descriptive passages to the next level.

It is all very well to describe what you see, hear, smell etc, but good description goes beyond that. You need to describe how it makes you *feel*.

In my book *Battlesaurus: Rampage at Waterloo*, the main character set off on a dangerous early morning trip into a forest. I could have simply described it like this:

> The sun was rising, bringing a red glow to the grey sky above the misty forest.

That would have been adequate, but it does not evoke feeling. Here is what I actually wrote:

> The dawn sky is a cold grey pan of gruel, coloured only by a creeping redness to the east, like dripping blood diffusing in a bowl of dirty water. As it spreads, it reveals a morning ground-fog choking the trees of the forest.

Did you notice my deliberate use of the words 'cold', 'creeping', 'dripping blood' and 'choking' to evoke the dangers that lie ahead.

If you are writing a descriptive passage, I want you to first see it in your mind, as vividly as you can. Then stop thinking about it, listen instead to your heart, your feelings. Let your subconscious come up with words to express those emotions and write them down, even if they don't make perfect sense.

After that you can re-engage your brain and work on the words you have written. Make sure that they do make sense and that it conveys what you are trying to convey to the reader. Show it to your writing buddy. See if they get the same feelings that you did.

> Good writing is supposed to evoke sensation in the reader – not the fact that it is raining, but the feeling of being rained upon.
> – E.L. Doctorow

MY STORY

I am playing around with some descriptions of Jason's apartment building. I will include these in a scene where he goes to search for his sistter. Here is what I have so far:

> Our apartment building is an old one. Thirteen stories of concrete, stained by years of bird-poo, dwarfed by shiny new metal and mirror-glass apartments on three sides. The fourth side looks over a small park and playground.
> I avoid the elevator, a creaky old dear with metal cage doors you have to close by hand. Instead I use the stairwell: decaying concrete with rusting handrails. It smells of rot and pee.

That's a start, although I am not sure I am really 'feeling' this yet. I will keep working on it.

Description Exercise

Take one of these three lines of narration.

1. The small fish swam into the rusted cannon barrel of the sunken warship just before the shark cruised past.

2. I hid in the darkest corner of the dungeon as the mad prince approached, flaming torch in one hand, dagger in the other.

3. Noah didn't expect to spend that day hiding in the darkened janitor's cupboard. But he did expect to be alone in there. He was wrong on both counts.

Add description to it.
Whichever one you chose, take a moment and let the scene fill your imagination. What can you see? What can you hear? What can you smell? Is it cold, warm, hot? Is the air muggy or dry? Is the water calm or rough? Can you taste anything?

Tip: Use the **rule of three** : pick three senses and use them to add description to the scenario.

Write your descriptive passage here:

```
                                                              
                                                              
                                                              
                                                              
                                                              
                                                              
```

Now share it with your writing buddy. What is good about it? How could it be improved? Does it make you feel you are really there?

BRIAN SAYS

Remember to make the description match the mood or 'tone' of the story. Think about how your character is feeling then use description to show that to the reader.

For example: which of these two descriptive sentences would best suit the dungeon story?

The torch crackled and spat sharp slivers of flame, impaling the lurking shadows.

OR

Light danced freely on the breeze through the bars of the window, bringing with it the scent of rain on the fresh fields outside.

You would probably use the first example to help convey the terror that the prisoner feels as the mad prince approaches.

(You could use the second example to make a contrast between the dark, horrible cell, and the world outside.)

Dialogue

Writing convincing dialogue

Dialogue in books and movies is supposed to sound like conversation in real life. Except it isn't. Real life conversation is full of starts and stops and people talking over the top of each other and cutting each other off and changing subject without warning.

Dialogue in stories should sound like its real, but needs to be much more focussed.
Making dialogue tight and interesting is hard. I have a whole section devoted to this in the **Special Ops** workbook.

Here are four simple ways to help write great dialogue.

1. Write your dialogue separately. On a separate document, leave out all the description and other stuff and just write each character's name and what they say, as if you were writing a play. This allows you to focus on just the spoken bits. Later, mix it back into your story.

2. Act it out. Gather some friends and read out the dialogue. Don't just read it, act it. If a character is angry, be angry; if they are sad, be sad. See what works, and what seems clumsy or stilted. Rewrite the weak bits and do it all again.

3. Use Character Visualisation. Find pictures of your characters. Search the internet for photos of your characters. They might be your friends, or movie stars, or just random people, but they are how you picture your characters in your mind. Print the photos out, and when writing their dialogue, stare at the pictures and imagine them talking to each other.

4. Simplify it. How can you say what needs to be said in fewer words. Remove any unnecessary fluff (unless it is important for the voice of the character).

Make sure you read about formatting dialogue on page 19 & 20.

BRIAN SAYS

Readers love to be surprised. If your character says exactly what the reader expects them to say, it can be a little boring. So try to make your characters say things that are unexpected. For example:

"Hey dad, can I borrow the car?" Ryan asked.
"Where are you going and when will you be back?" his father asked.

That's a predictable response to the question. But what if the conversation went something like this:

"Hey dad, can I borrow the car?" Ryan asked.
"How's Katrina," his father asked. "You two still fighting?"

Now I don't know where the dad is going with that Katrina question, but neither does the reader, so it is less predictable and more interesting. Of course it must all tie back in to Ryan's question at some stage.

Copyright 2016, Brian Falkner - 13

Action

Action doesn't necessarily means guns, explosions and martial arts fighting (although it can be that too). It simply means that a character in your story does something.
They might drive their car, open a door or write an email.
The trick when writing action is to include only the important actions that make a difference to the story.
Your reader is a busy person. You don't want to waste their time telling them lots of unnecessary detail.

Action Exercise

Can you simplify this series of actions to a single sentence?

> Lara opened the cupboard and took out a cup. She placed it on the bench. She put some water in the kettle and turned it on to start boiling. She opened another cupboard and found a box of tea bags. She opened the box and took out a tea bag. She closed the box and put it back in the cupboard. She put the tea bag in the cup. The water finished boiling and she picked up the kettle. She carefully poured some water into the cup then replaced the kettle on the stand. She held the little cardboard tag of the tea bag and jiggled it up and down, watching the tea get darker and darker. When it was dark enough she took the tea bag out and put it in the trash. She went to the fridge and got out a bottle of milk. She poured some into the tea until the colour was right, then put the milk back in the fridge.

Write your sentence here:

....

....

Unless you are doing it deliberately to create suspense (more on that in workbook four), always simplify actions, keep them tight and as short as possible.

MY STORY

If you have a long section of dialogue with absolutely vital information, you can make it more interesting by interspersing it with some actions.

Two people standing around talking is boring. Get them doing stuff.

In my story there will be two police officers who are asking questions about the missing girl.

I am going to give them some interesting things to do. I am not sure what yet. Perhaps something unexpected, like chewing gum during the interview.

Inner Thoughts

How can we really know what your character is feeling if we don't know what they are thinking.

On the other hand, we don't want to hear every thought they think. You have to judge when it will help the reader to know what the character is thinking, and when it would be better to keep their thoughts private.

You will probably make more use of inner thoughts if you are writing in the *First Person* Point of View, rather than *Third Person*. There's more detail about Point of View on the next page but basically *First Person* is when you say 'I' a lot.

> I went to the store and bought a sandwich.

Third person is when you say 'he' or 'she' a lot.

> John went to the store and bought a sandwich.

In *First Person* Point of View the reader is already much more inside the narrator's head, because it is the narrator who is telling the story. So it seems more natural for the narrator to say what they are thinking.

With third person, because it is like watching someone else do things, it does not feel as natural to hear their thoughts, so it is wise to do it less often.

The doorway to the mind is always open in the written story. Since we can go inside, we must go inside. If we don't, it will always feel as if something is missing.
— Jerry Cleaver

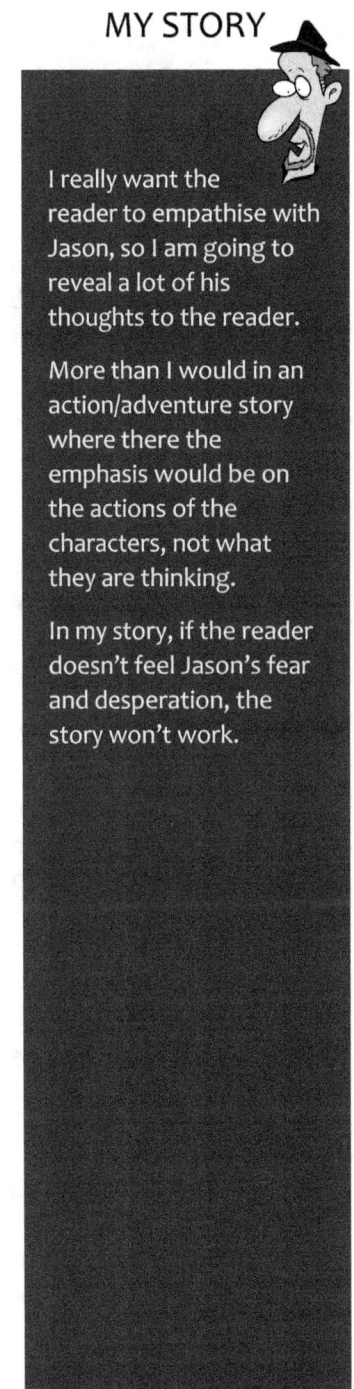

MY STORY

I really want the reader to empathise with Jason, so I am going to reveal a lot of his thoughts to the reader.

More than I would in an action/adventure story where there the emphasis would be on the actions of the characters, not what they are thinking.

In my story, if the reader doesn't feel Jason's fear and desperation, the story won't work.

POV and Tense

You have a lot of choices to make when you start a story. One is the point of view (who is telling the story). Another decision is tense (past or present). POV and tense can make a huge difference to a story.

First person (*I did, I said*) feels much closer to the reader than third person (*he did, she said*). But you can only write about things that the main character experiences directly.

Third person allows a wider view of the story. You can tell the reader about different things happening to different people.

Present tense can feel more immediate, as though something is happening right now, rather than telling about something that happened in the past.

Past tense is more flexible. You can tell about different things that happened at different times. It is more common that present tense and many readers feel more comfortable with it.

Here is a passage from *The Super Freak* in third person, past tense.

> They crossed over the racing track and were following a dusty metal road that led away from it when Fizzer heard the pick-up truck. At first he thought that help was at hand, but then realised that the noise was coming from behind them.
> "Get off the road!" Fizzer said urgently.
> Tupai, who had heard nothing, obeyed without question.

Here it is rewritten in first person, present tense.

> We cross over the racing track and are following a dusty metal road that leads away from it when I hear the pick-up truck. At first I think that help is at hand, but then I realise that the noise is coming from behind us.
> "Get off the road!" I say urgently.
> Tupai obeys without question.

There is no hard and fast rule about which one to use. I suggest you read the two passages above and use them to help you decide which tense and POV you want to use for your story.

MY STORY

There are four choices for tense and POV. They are:

1. First person, present
2. First person, past
3. Third person, present
4. Third person, past

I have decided to use first person, present for my story.

I like the direct connection it has to the reader, and also the immediacy of using the present tense.

We experience the story at the same time as the main character. His desperate search for his sister is happening as we read about it.

A note:

Some authors mix POVs. James Patterson often intersperses chapters in first person with ones in third person. (I don't recommend this. You have to be very skilled to make this work.)

Copyright 2016, Brian Falkner

Momentum

Before we even start writing I want to talk to you about how to keep your writing moving. How to maintain your momentum and to avoid the dreadful feeling of not knowing to write next.

You might be stuck for a story idea, a line of dialogue, or even just a word. Some people call this *"Writer's Block"*.

The best way to overcome writer's block is to write. Write something. Write anything. If you're not sure what happens next, but you know what happens after that, then **write the bit you know.** You can go back and fill in the gap later.

The worst thing you can do is to stop writing, because that way the blank page starts to look more and more insurmountable. This doesn't mean you can't stop for a little bit. Sometimes a walk, a lie-down, a cup of coffee, is all it takes to shake up your creative bits and get them working again.

When your writing is flowing, its exciting and fun. When you get stuck, its hard. It takes a lot of effort and discipline to keep motivated and to keep writing.

Here's one way to avoid getting stuck in the middle of a story.

I call it **STAR POWER!**

BRIAN SAYS

Most writers I know (including me) have gone through times of intense self-doubt where they felt they had lost the ability to write and would never complete another story.

This is so common that I suspect it is part of the creative process.

It is usually followed by a stage where the writer produces what they consider to be their best ever work.

For me this happened after I finished my Recon Team Angel series and the book that followed was *Battlesaurus: Rampage at Waterloo*.

The difference between dreams and reality... ...is called discipline
- Unknown

* Star Power!*

I often get stuck on something trivial. A word; a name; a turn of phrase. I found I could waste a lot of time trying to solve that problem, and meanwhile the flow of my writing stopped. My momentum came to a halt. So I developed a technique of marking difficult bits with six stars like this ******, and moving on. I finish my sentence; my page; my chapter.

Of course it's not quite finished because I still have to go back and fix up all the gaps where I left the stars. But it is much easier to go back and tackle those problems one by one after I have finished the section I am working on.

When I am finished, I use the search function in my word processor to look for ******. It finds the first one, I work on it until I have sorted it out, then I keep going. Here is an example. It is an excerpt from my book *Maddy West and the Tongue Taker*.

> Some houses, to Maddy, seemed to be happy, with fresh paint and ******. Other houses seemed dour and sullen, watching you go by with a sour expression. Yet other houses seemed sad and tired, especially those ones all crammed together in long rows on long dreary streets.
>
> This house looked mean. It looked angry. ****** Maddy thought as they bounced up a long winding, and ****** driveway through ****** gardens that had gone to rot and ruin. ******.

And here it is again, after I went back and filled in all the * gaps

> Some houses, to Maddy, seemed to be happy, with fresh paint and bright windows like smiling eyes and little lace curtains puffing gently in the breeze.
>
> Other houses seemed dour and sullen, watching you go by with a sour expression. Yet other houses seemed sad and tired, especially those ones all crammed together in long rows on long dreary streets.
>
> This house looked mean. It looked angry. Perhaps ferocious was the right word to use, Maddy thought as they bounced up a long winding, and decrepit driveway through dark and overgrown gardens that had gone to rot and ruin. Black vines and creepers twisted their way up around trees and plants, strangling them.

******

Why six stars?

Because sometimes when I am going through my novel, searching for the ****** I find one that I still can't fix. I don't want to get stuck, so I remove one star and move on.

When I search for 6 stars I won't find any marked with 5 stars.

I finish that edit, and start again from the beginning.

This time I search for 5 stars.

*****

Any I am still stuck on, I remove one more star.

****

And so on.

***

And so on.

**

Formatting

It is important to format the text of your story in a way that makes it easy to read. To show you what a difference it makes, here is a short excerpt from *The Project* unformatted, then formatted.

UNFORMATTED

> "We would have got away with it if it wasn't for that drunken squirrel," said Luke. He managed a grin at Tommy, sitting next to him on the hard slatted bench outside the vice principal's office. As always, in the cold, hard light of the next day, their prank seemed childish and stupid. But this time Luke had discovered the universal law of vice-principals: those in America had no better sense of humour than those back in New Zealand. "Don't sweat it, dude," Tommy said. "I can handle Kerr." "Yeah right." Tommy's dad was a lawyer, and Tommy always thought he could talk his way out of anything. Sometimes he was right. Tommy had a coin in his hand and was flipping it up in the air, catching it first on the top side of his fingers, then the underside. "Seriously," he said. "I've been in more courtrooms than you've had hot dinners. I'm going to tie this sucker up in so many legal knots that he'll look like a pretzel."

FORMATTED

> "We would have got away with it if it wasn't for that drunken squirrel," said Luke.
>
> He managed a grin at Tommy, sitting next to him on the hard slatted bench outside the vice principal's office.
>
> As always, in the cold, hard light of the next day, their prank seemed childish and stupid. But this time Luke had discovered the universal law of vice-principals: those in America had no better sense of humour than those back in New Zealand.
>
> "Don't sweat it, dude," Tommy said. "I can handle Kerr."
>
> "Yeah right."
>
> Tommy's dad was a lawyer, and Tommy always thought he could talk his way out of anything. Sometimes he was right.
>
> Tommy had a coin in his hand and was flipping it up in the air, catching it first on the top side of his fingers, then the underside.
>
> "Seriously," he said. "I've been in more courtrooms than you have had hot dinners. I'm going to tie this sucker up in so many legal knots that he'll look like a pretzel."

BRIAN SAYS

See how much easier it is to read the formatted version?

You could write the best story in the world, but nobody might ever read it if you don't format it properly.

Unformatted text is really hard to read, and a reader might just give up before they really get into your story.

Learn how to format text and do it as you go.

Then when you are editing your story, check that you have done it correctly.

Formatting Text

Here are some very simple rules to help you format your story:

- Start a new paragraph if you change location in the story.
- Start a new paragraph whenever something new happens (a new event).
- Start a new paragraph whenever a new person starts talking.
- Indent paragraphs (or put a blank line between them) to make it easy to see where the paragraph begins and ends.
- Put quotation marks (" ") around dialogue.
- End the dialogue with a comma, close the quotes, then add a speech tag. (There are some other options for dialogue, see below).

Speech Tags

A speech tag is that little bit you add to dialogue to let the reader know who was talking. For example *'he said'* or *'she says'*.

> "You usually put this at the end," Brian says.
> Brian says, "However you can also put it at the beginning."
> "Sometimes you put it in the middle," Brian says, "to break up a long sentence."

"Said" (or "Says") is your basic speech tag. Use this wherever possible.

Unless you need to use something different for clarity, such as *she whispered*, or *he shouted*, just stick with 'she said'.

(I know your English teacher might encourage you to use other words like 'exclaimed, mumbled, etc' but professional authors try to avoid these words. They distract the reader from the dialogue.)

Now go back and look at the examples on the previous page to see these rules in action.

MY STORY

Sometimes you can avoid using speech tags, but only do this if it is obvious who is talking.

Here are some lines of dialogue between Jason and his mother that I am playing around with for my story. Can you tell who is speaking?

"I'm going to look for her," I say.
"No you're not!"
"Mum, I can't do nothing!"
"I'm not doing nothing," she says as if my comment is a dig at her.
"I won't go out of the building," I say.
"The police will do the searching, you stay here," she says.
"No!"
"Yes! I don't want to risk losing both of you."
"You won't," I say.
"Then I'd have nobody," she says in a voice suddenly tired and quiet.

Research and World Building

In the same way that you need to create and build up your characters, you need to build the world they will inhabit.

If your story was set on a submarine, for example, you would need to know everything there was to know about submarines, how they operate, the people who crew them and so on. You would need to be able to describe the surroundings, as well as the procedures and know the commands and routines of life on board.

Fortunately, thanks to the internet, research is not as hard as it used to be.

If your story was set on a fictional spaceship, you need to work even harder to make up all the stuff you need to know, because you can't research photos, videos, or read accounts from people who have been there.

You must know all about the world in your story, and build a rich, vivid experience for the readers who will come to visit. This applies whether your setting is a school, a fantasy world, or your house.

This doesn't mean you have to use all that information in your story. If you research properly and know the world well, it will show through in small details that you add to your writing. The way in which a sailor opens a submarine hatch, the small creatures that scuttle around in the undergrowth on a new planet. A few small touches here and there that paint a picture and show that you really know this world intimately.

Just as characters must seem real to the reader, so must the world where they live.

BRIAN SAYS

I research as thoroughly as I can. When possible, I will travel to the different locations in my story, to experience them first hand.

I went to New York and Las Vegas for *Brainjack*; to the Bay of Islands (New Zealand) for *The Tomorrow Code*; and to the outback of Australia for *Assault*.

If I can't visit a location I use the internet. Especially Google Earth and Street View. I will search for photographs of locations, and read accounts from people who have visited there.

That's definitely second best though. Nothing beats standing in a place, breathing in the air; smelling the smells; hearing the sounds; watching the people; drinking in the whole atmosphere of a place.

Getting Started

Sometimes the hardest part of writing is just getting started.

This is where all the hard work you did in *Basic Training* is going to pay off.

Go back and look at your outline for your story. Look at the storyboard you made. That should give you a big clue as to what you are going to write first.

You are probably going to introduce the main character, usually involved in some kind of action that reveals a bit of their personality and circumstances. And very quickly you are going to bring on the trigger, that will kick off the events of your story.

Some ways to start a story:

Dialogue. You can start with one of the characters talking. Some writers don't like this, but I think it can be effective.

> "Where's papa going with that axe," said Fern to her mother as they were setting the table for breakfast. (Charlotte's web)

An **action**. This is a powerful way to start a story.

> A bamboo bowl flew through the air, aimed at the slave girl's head. (Dragon Keeper).

Narration. There is no harm in a quick bit of narration to get the story moving.

> These two very old people are the father and mother of Mr Bucket. (Charlie and the Chocolate Factory)

Description can work too, as long as it doesn't go on too long and bore the reader.

> The hottest day of summer so far was drawing to a close and a drowsy silence lay over the large, square houses of Privet Drive. (Harry Potter and the order of the Phoenix).

Once you have your first few sentences sorted out, focus on how you will get to the trigger and get your story started.

MY STORY

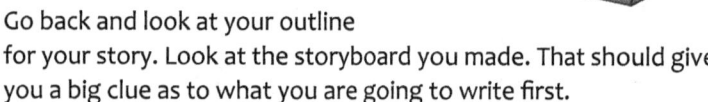

I want to hit the reader straight up with the problem. Jason's sister has disappeared.

Now I need a way to reveal this that won't seem like 'telling'. I want to 'show' the reader the problem.

I might be able to do this with the police officers who interview Jason and his mother about the disappearance.

Maybe I won't reveal at first the truth of why the police officers are there. That will create some mystery from the outset.

How Jason and his mother react to the police officers could be quite revealing of their characters.

One of the officers could ask something like:

"When was the last time you saw your sister alive?"

Rewriting ~~and Editing~~

After you finish your first draft you might think you have finished your story. Wrong! You have only just begun. The real hard work and the real magic comes in the rewriting. That's where you take the raw, rough words of your first draft and shape them into something awesome.

My first advice? Print your story out, and edit it on paper using a pen. Why? I don't know. And all authors are different, so this might not work for you, but I see the story differently when it is printed. I have new ideas. I see things I would not have seen otherwise. There is something different about the printed page.
(I am working on a printed copy of this page right now.)

After you finish, incorporate your changes back into your document on your computer or device. This can be another chance to find mistakes and make improvements.

As you edit your story, make sure you follow these steps:

- Compare what you wrote to the Three Act Story Structure (See *Basic Training*). Go through your story and make sure you have all the parts in all the right places.

- Can you tighten up your **narration?** Do you repeat yourself or use unnecessary words?

- Are your **descriptions** vivid, but not too flowery?

- Do your **characters** shine through their **dialogue** and **actions?**

- Does each character's **voice** (the way they speak) match their age, background and personality.

- Check your **formatting,** along with your spelling and grammar.

I am writing a FIRST DRAFT, and reminding myself that I am simply shoveling sand into a box ...

...so that later I can build CASTLES
— Shannon Hale

BRIAN SAYS

On the next page is the raw, unedited first page of my story.

In the next workbook, *Ticking Time Bombs*, I look at how to create and develop suspense and tension in your story.

In that workbook I have put an edited version of the same first page of my story, so you can see the kind of changes I make when editing.

PS. I have left one deliberate error on this this page. Can you find it?

My Story

Here is the start of my story. This has not yet been edited. I'll do that in the next workbook, Ticking Time Bombs.

"When was the last time you saw your sister alive?"
The question, once asked, cannot be un-asked even when the young policewoman realises what she has said and rephrases it quickly.
"When was the last time you saw your sister?"
I know the answer, because I have been thinking about it all morning. Tumbling it all over in my head till it is driving me insane.

The last time I saw Charli was when she went to bed. She was being naughty. Mum was getting stressed, so I went to sort it out. Most days, sorting family stuff out seems to be my job. I guess that's fair. I am the oldest.

Dad does it when he is here, which is like, never.

"She wouldn't go to sleep," I say. "Whenever I turned her light out, she turned it back on."

"How?" the other police-person asks. He is a big bear of a man with a short beard. He unwraps a stick of gum and starts chewing.

"There's a switch by the door, and one by the bed," I explain and the policeman nods.

"Did your mother not tell her off?" the policewoman asks.

"She was busy," I say.

I can't look at mum when I say that so I stare at the picture on the wall behind them. A painting of a young lady drinking a glass of soda through a straw. The glass is cold and frosted and it always makes me feel thirsty. Especially today. My throat is a desert. The gap where my missing tooth is feels dry and hard.

The police-people stay for another hour, asking lots of questions and examining Charli's room. Violet curtains, violet bedspread, a teddy-bear with a violet waistcoat. Quite neat and tidy, even the bed is made. But that's just Charli. She hates mess.

Mum seems relieved when the police-people leave. Not relieved that they are gone, but relieved that the problem is now out of her hands. Professionals are on the case.

I am not so convinced. They don't know where to start looking. They don't know anything.

They don't have a clue.

BRIAN SAYS

We are nearly there!

That's the end of this writing workbook.

The fourth workbook is about creating suspense and tension in your stories.

In other words, how to keep the reader on the edge of their seat!

See you there!

Quotes about Writing

Throughout this workbook I have sprinkled some of my favourite quotations from famous authors about writing. Here are a few more.

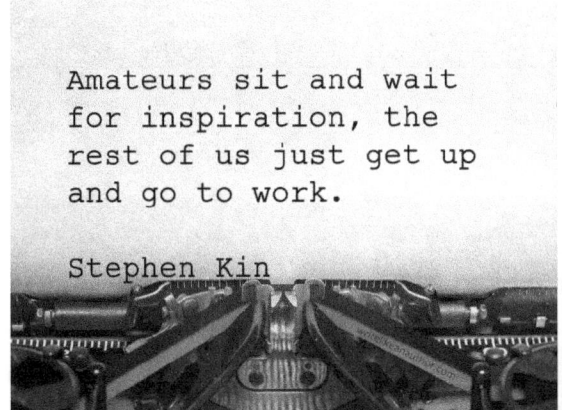

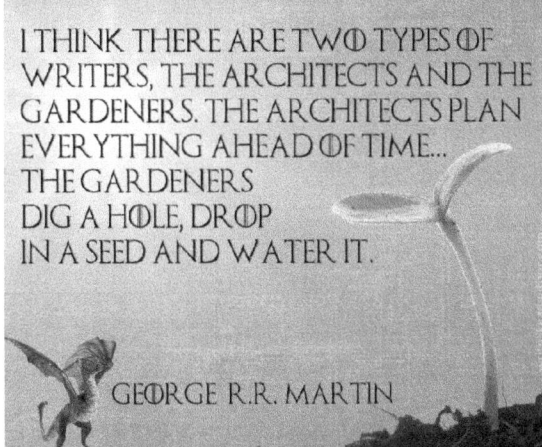

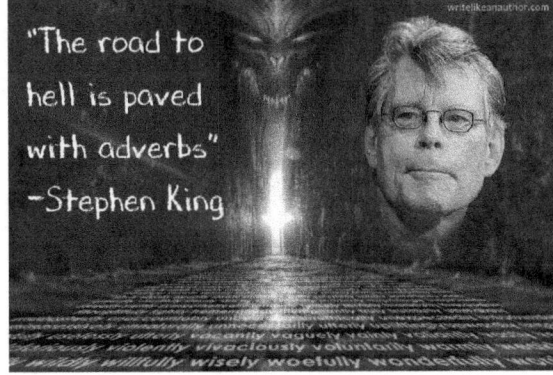

Course Notes:

www.ingramcontent.com/pod-product-compliance
Lightning Source LLC
La Vergne TN
LVHW081528060526
838200LV00045B/2044